Larry Ellison
Database Genius of Oracle

INTERNET BIOGRAPHIES

BILL GATES
Software Genius of Microsoft
0-7660-1969-1

LARRY ELLISON
Database Genius of Oracle
0-7660-1974-8

ESTHER DYSON
Internet Visionary
0-7660-1973-X

STEVE CASE
Internet Genius of America Online
0-7660-1971-3

JEFF BEZOS
Business Genius of Amazon.com
0-7660-1972-1

STEVE JOBS
Computer Genius of Apple
0-7660-1970-5

INTERNET BIOGRAPHIES

Larry Ellison
Database Genius of Oracle

by Craig Peters

Enslow Publishers, Inc.

40 Industrial Road   PO Box 38
Box 398   Aldershot
Berkeley Heights, NJ 07922   Hants GU12 6BP
USA   UK

http://www.enslow.com

PRODUCED BY:
Chestnut Productions
Russell, Massachusetts

Editor and Picture Researcher: *Mary E. Hull*
Design and Production: *Lisa Hochstein*

Library of Congress Cataloging-in-Publication Data

Peters, Craig, 1958-
  Larry Ellison : database genius of Oracle / by Craig Peters.
      p. cm. — (Internet biographies)
Summary: Explores the life and career of the billionaire businessman who co-founded the Oracle software company, discussing his accomplishments in the computing and Internet worlds.
Includes bibliographical references and index.
  ISBN 0-7660-1974-8
  1. Ellison, Larry—Juvenile literature. 2. Businessmen—United States—Biography—Juvenile literature. 3. Computer software industry—United States—Juvenile literature. 4. Oracle Corporation—History—Juvenile literature. [1. Ellison, Larry. 2. Businesspeople. 3. Computer software industry. 4. Oracle Corporation—History.] I. Title. II. Series.
HD9696.63.U62 E446 2003
338.7'610053'092—dc21
                                                    2002153180

Printed in the United States of America

10 9 8 7 6 5 4 3 2 1

To Our Readers:
We have done our best to make sure all Internet addresses in this book were active and appropriate when we went to press. However, the author and the publisher have no control over and assume no liability for the material available on those Internet sites or on other Web sites they may link to. Any comments or suggestions can be sent by e-mail to comments@enslow.com or to the address on the back cover.

Opposite Title Page: *Larry Ellison was able to report a surge in Oracle's profits for 2000. The surge came from increased sales of the company's database and e-business software.*

CONTENTS

Sayonara lost a sail at the start of the Sydney-to-Hobart race. The crew managed to replace the triangular sail, called a spinnaker. They also maintained their lead over the fleet of 115 yachts.

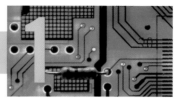

High Drama on the High Seas

L arry Ellison is the co-founder of the Oracle Corporation, which produces Oracle software. Ellison is also a billionaire. And he likes to tackle the unknown. Ellison uses determination to succeed at whatever he tries.

In December, 1998, he was aboard his racing yacht, *Sayonara*. He and twenty-four crew members were competing in Australia's Sydney-to-Hobart yacht race. This famous ocean race began in 1945. It takes sailors from Sydney, Australia, across the Bass Strait to Hobart, a town on the island of Tasmania. There were 115 yachts in the 1998 race. *Sayonora* was a favorite to win. Ellison predicted *Sayonara* would win. He also boasted it would set a new world record for the 725-mile course.

As the race got underway, *Sayonara* was in a close three-way battle for the lead. Then, bad weather erupted. Before long, *Sayonara* was sailing in the worst storm ever in the fifty-four year history of the race.

Ellison described what it was like on board during the storm:

> You'd just bury yourself in the wave. It was like going up an elevator. Normally, the dangerous part of a wave is sliding down the back. You start surfing. You can actually turn side-on and roll the boat. But we didn't have that problem. The back of the wave was so steep that you'd just exit the wave and fall straight down like a ball in an elevator shaft—one, one thousand; two, one thousand; three, one thousand. Crash! It was like being dropped off a four-story building onto asphalt every forty-five seconds. That happened for three hours. It was very bad.[1]

But *Sayonara* stayed the course. It built a firm lead. *Sayonara* was sailing on a pace to set a world record. Then, the weather got worse. The winds went from fifty miles per hour to one hundred miles per hour. Fifty foot waves—nearly four stories high—battered the vessels. Helicopters pulled dozens of sailors out of the roaring ocean. It was the largest sea rescue in Australian history. Six sailors drowned. Seventy-one boats quit the race due to the bad weather. Seven yachts were abandoned. Five boats sank.

Ellison's *Sayonara* was the first yacht to arrive at the dock in Hobart. Ellison was visibly shaken. There was little joy in winning a race in which six men had died.

Spectator craft fill Sydney Harbor at the start of the 1998 Sydney-to-Hobart ocean race on December 26. Stormy weather plagued the boats during the 725-mile race.

"It was just awful. I've never experienced anything remotely like this," Ellison said. "It's been a very emotional experience to get here. This is not what this is supposed to be about."[2]

"Never again. Not if I live to be 1,000 years old will I do a Hobart race," Ellison added.

It was truly extraordinary to the extreme. Anyone who signs up for this race expects a difficult race, but no one expects a dangerous race. It was extremely dangerous out there. The seas were enormous. The wind made sounds I've never heard before.[3]

THE ELLISON STYLE

Larry Ellison's strong personality helped him navigate the stormy seas off the coast of Australia. It has helped him succeed in big business, too. Many people did not like him.

For example, Ellison once rewarded ruthless employees by paying them in gold coins. He wanted his workers to be loyal to him no matter what happened. One of his employees left to start Siebel Systems, a software business that competed with Oracle. Ellison may have wanted to get even by luring some employees away from Siebel. He sent an ice cream truck to Siebel Systems. He had the driver hand out free ice cream sandwiches to the employees. The wrappers on the ice cream sandwiches read: "Summer is near. Oracle is here. To brighten your day and your career."[4]

Ellison was known for landing his $38 million Gulfstream V private jet after hours at the San Jose, California, airport. To cut down on noise, the airport forbid heavy planes from taking off or landing between 11:30 P.M. and 6:30 A.M. But Ellison preferred to land on his own schedule. After he had violated the curfew nine times, the city threatened to sue him. But Ellison said his plane was quieter than other lighter planes. He sued San Jose for the right to fly when he wanted to, and he won.

Ellison did some other things that shocked people. He paid $40 million to have his home custom-made in Japan then assembled on his estate in California. But he did not care what people thought about his home or business. "When everyone else says we are crazy," Ellison said, "I say, 'Gee, we must really be on to something.'"[5]

One year later Ellison reflected on his brush with death. "I'll never forget the experience," he said. "It was incredible. But . . . have I changed my life? Do I do things differently? No. Not really."[6]

Ellison stared death in the face and came away believing he was unchanged. This supreme confidence has been a life-long trait of Ellison's.

This aerial view shows what downtown Chicago looked like when Larry Ellison was growing up there in the 1940s.

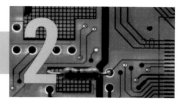
Humble Beginnings

L awrence Joseph Ellison was born August 17, 1944, in New York City. His mother, Florence, was a single mom. She was only nineteen years old when he was born.

By age one, Larry had already struggled through a bout of pneumonia. He had a severe case and almost died. Florence was struggling, too. It was hard to make ends meet as a single working mother on the lower east side of Manhattan.

"She thought it would be a good idea if she gave me up," Ellison said. "She couldn't work and care for a child. It was difficult."[1]

Larry was sent to live with his mother's aunt, Lillian Ellison, and her husband, Louis. They lived in a Jewish neighborhood on the South Side of Chicago.

"I remember *Look* magazine called [Chicago's South Side] the oldest and worst black ghetto in the United States," Ellison recalled.

When Larry Ellison was a boy, personal computers did not exist yet. The first personal computer was sold by International Business Machines (IBM) in 1981.

> It was a lower-middle class neighborhood . . . A Jewish ghetto. It was surrounded by a black ghetto and a Puerto Rican and Latino ghetto. But it wasn't anything like the ghettos today. I mean, the ghettos of today . . . are dominated by guns and drugs. I didn't even know I lived in a 'bad' neighborhood. I was unaware of it. No one told me. And I didn't discover it until I left.[2]

Larry was an average student in high school. He enjoyed playing basketball, though he never played on the school team. He played ball with neighborhood kids.

In 1962, Ellison graduated from Chicago's South Shore High School. He enrolled at the University of

Illinois. At first he thought he might become a doctor, but he changed his mind. In his junior year, he switched to the University of Chicago. He took a part-time programming job with the university. He taught himself how to program the computers. "I never took a computer science class in my life," Ellison recalled in 1995. "I just picked up a book and started programming."[3] Before long, Ellison left the University of Chicago, too. In the summer of 1966, he traveled to California.

"The very things that caused me to fail in school have made me successful in life," Ellison told *Business Week* in February, 2001.

> I have always had difficulty with conventional wisdom. So teachers would say certain things—and I wouldn't necessarily believe what they had to say. Just because they said it, and they were experts, and they were in authority did not automatically mean they were right.
>
> It created problems between me and my parents at times. And between me and my teachers, and me and my peers. But in the end, when you go out into the real world, it's when you find errors in conventional wisdom—when everyone says A is true, and A is not true—that you gain your competitive advantage. Only a few times do you have to find errors in conventional wisdom to make a living.[4]

Ellison arrived in northern California, broke and in need of a job. He took a job at an employment agency. He met a woman named Adda Quinn, and they began dating. Ellison and Quinn were married on January 23, 1967.

During this time, Ellison did some computer-related work for a variety of companies. Mostly, though, he bounced from job to job.

"The financial stresses were Adda's," Ellison said. "They weren't mine. She had a program, you know? Get promoted, have an ambition, go do something. That's just the way the world is. And I was perfectly happy to do a little writing [and] play the guitar."[5] Larry and Adda divorced in 1974.

Ellison took a job with the Amdahl Corporation. They built large computers used to store information

A LOVE OF JAPANESE CULTURE

Ellison's employer, Amdahl, was owned in part by the Japanese company Fujitsu. Amdahl employees sometimes traveled to Japan. It was there that Ellison fell in love with Japanese culture.

"I took a business trip to Japan and while there visited the city of Kyoto," Ellison said in 1995. "And I was stunned; it was one of only two times I was stunned. The first time was when I saw Yosemite Valley. I simply didn't know such a thing could exist. The same thing [happened] with Kyoto."[6]

for businesses. These computers are called mainframes. Their competition was a company called International Business Machines (IBM). At the time, many people believed that IBM would become the leader in the developing computer industry. They spent a lot of money on research. Because Ellison had worked with IBM computers, he was hired to teach engineers at Amdahl about them.

"I can recall running out of money between paychecks," he said, "and living on macaroni and cheese and rice. But I didn't take money very seriously until my late twenties [when] I wanted to buy a house. I thought: If only I had a house—I had never lived in a house before. I'd figure out some way to make enough money to get a house."[7]

Before long, money would be the least of Larry Ellison's worries.

Larry Ellison got the idea for his company, Oracle, while researching ways for computers to store information.

The Creation of Oracle

The Amdahl Corporation was struggling in 1973. To cut costs, it decided to get rid of some employees. Larry Ellison was let go from the company, but it wound up being a fortunate turn of events for him.

Ellison got a programming job at Ampex, a maker of audio and video equipment. There he met two people who would change the course of his life. The first was Bob Miner, a manager in the Ampex programming department.

"I thought that my manager, the manager they assigned me to, was not technically competent," Ellison said. "So I refused to work for him. So I said, 'I'll work for Bob. He's the best guy. I'll work for him.'"[1]

The second influential person Ellison met was Edward Oates, an Ampex programmer. On his second day of work at Ampex, Oates heard Ellison mention his ex-wife's name. In a remarkable bit of coincidence,

When Ellison began working for Ampex in the 1970s, computers stored data on large spools of tape like the ones shown above. It was time-consuming to access information stored on the tapes.

it turned out that Adda Quinn and Edward Oates had gone to high school together.

Miner, Ellison, and Oates worked together on a project called "Oracle." Their job was to find a way for computers to store and quickly access large amounts of information. In the mid-1970s, computers stored data on large spools of magnetic tape. This tape was like the kind of tape found inside a videocassette. The tapes could store a lot of information. Accessing the information, however, was a slow and awkward process.

Ampex tried to create a high-speed tape system. Ellison, Miner, and Oates worked on writing the software programs that could make the system work.

Before long, however, they realized that the system would not work. Ellison left Ampex to become vice president of Systems Development for a company called Precision Instrument. Like Ampex, Precision Instrument was working on a system for storing and retrieving large amounts of information.

Precision Instrument had a machine, but it had no software for that machine. That's where Ellison saw an opportunity. He contacted Miner and Oates and convinced them that they should start a company. The company's first contract would be to write the software that Precision Instrument needed. Software Development Laboratories, later called Oracle, was born in June, 1977.

At the time, Miner was named president of the new company. Oates was vice president. Ellison, who had the idea to start the company in the first place, continued working for Precision Instrument. His job was to oversee the work that Software Development Laboratories was doing.

There were big developments in Ellison's personal life around this time, too. He'd met Nancy Elizabeth Wheeler in 1976, and they were soon married. But the couple divorced in July, 1978, after only a year and a half together.

At about the same time, the research department of IBM published a paper called "The System R Project." The paper described an attempt to create a relational database. A relational database is a way to store information in complex ways. IBM also published information about a special computer programming language. The language could be used to write programs for a relational database. It was called structured query language, or SQL, and pronounced just like the word "sequel."

Ellison saw an opportunity. "In November of 1976, I saw the paper, and thought that, on the basis of this research, we could build a commercial system," he recalled in 1995. "And, in fact, if we were clever, we could take IBM's research, build the commercial system, and beat IBM to the marketplace with this technology. Because we thought we could move faster than they could."[2]

WHAT'S IN A NAME?

Where did the name "Oracle" come from?

Larry Ellison, Bob Miner, and Edward Oates took the name from a project they worked on together at Ampex for the Central Intelligence Agency (CIA). The CIA is a government agency that works to protect the security of the United States. The word "oracle" means a person through whom a deity, or god, speaks, or a special place where hidden knowledge is revealed.

Since the goal of the project was to reveal the knowledge that was "hidden" in the mass of information held by a company or government organization, the name "Oracle" made sense for the new software.

And they did. Software Development Laboratories spent two years developing the first version of their database software. They named the software "Oracle" after the failed project that Ellison, Miner, and Oates had worked on at Ampex.

The first version of Oracle was sold and installed in November of 1979. The company was off and running. "We were profitable from the days we opened our doors," Ellison said.[3] In 1983, Software Development Laboratories renamed itself Oracle Corporation. Three years later, on March 12, 1986, Oracle went public. This meant that the company sold shares in

Traders at the New York Stock Exchange cluster around a post on the trading floor. Oracle sold its first shares of stock in 1986 for fifteen dollars a share.

WHAT IS A RELATIONAL DATABASE?

A database is simply an organized collection of information. Think of the following table as a small database of information for Family Number One:

NAME	AGE	BIRTHDAY
Craig	39	December 17
Barbara	39	November 11
Alexandra	13	March 7
Kyle	9	January 13

It is easy to look at the data and answer questions like, "How many children under the age of ten are in Family Number One?" But what if you had information like the above on a million families? Suppose you wanted to answer a question like, "How many children under the age of ten are named Kyle?" Obviously, that would be more difficult.

A relational database is able to answer these kinds of difficult questions very easily. That makes it a powerful tool for gathering information and knowledge. A relational database can store multiple tables of information. It can then create relationships among those tables. For the example above, one million tables might be created—one for each family. The software could then look through each of these tables and create a new one showing all the cases where the "AGE" is "less than ten" and the "NAME" is "Kyle."

The relational database was invented by E. F. Codd, a researcher at IBM, in 1970. A relational database allows businesses to gather, store, and use information much more quickly and efficiently than ever before.

the business to the public. The shares were then traded on the stock market.

One month later, Ellison filed for divorce from his third wife, Barbara Boothe. The couple had married in December 1983. They had two children, David and Margaret.

With three divorces in twelve years, Ellison's personal life was not a success. But his business life was. As the 1980s drew to a close, Oracle Corporation employed more than four thousand people worldwide. Its annual revenues approached $1 billion. The future looked as bright as could be.

Oracle's headquarters are located in Redwood City, California. Begun with just three employees in 1977, Oracle grew to employ more than forty-three thousand people by the beginning of the twenty-first century.

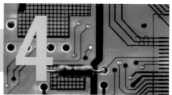

"The Internet Changes Everything"

O racle grew quickly during the first half of the 1990s. It introduced many new products. These products helped companies to manage their information with efficiency and speed. From 1990 to 1995, the company tripled its revenues. Ellison's personal fortune grew into the billions.

"When I started Oracle, what I wanted to do was create an environment where I would enjoy working," said Ellison. "That was my primary goal. Sure, I wanted to make a living. I certainly never expected to become rich, certainly not this rich. I mean, rich does not even describe this. This is surreal."[1]

Ellison used his wealth to learn how to fly exotic planes. He bought an unarmed Italian Marchetti S.211 fighter jet. He also bought a Gulfstream V jet for $38 million. On weekends he flew his planes over the Pacific Ocean.

Ellison enjoyed the lifestyle his wealth afforded him. He enjoyed his job—but not every day. On

In 2000, Oracle gave thousands of New Internet Computers, or NICs, to public schools as part of its $100 million program to furnish schools with new computers.

March 28, 1990, the company's stock price plunged from $25.38 per share to $17.50 per share. The stock price fell because Oracle announced that its profits were lower than expected. Oracle stockholders had to wait for the price of the stock to go back up before selling any, or risk losing a lot of money.

Big business means that you take the bad with the good, though. Oracle bounced back from its challenges and continued to grow.

By the mid-1990s, Larry Ellison was pushing a new idea. He proposed a shift from the personal computer (PC) to the network computer (NC). NCs were less expensive than PCs. They accessed information and programs from a mainframe computer instead of storing them on a large hard drive. They provided low-cost access to the Internet. Oracle hoped to provide the Internet-based software that would enable the NCs to operate. The drawback to NCs was that they could not do all the work that a PC could. But, as Ellison noted, most people did not need a powerful PC. "The PC is truly a marvel," he said, "but it's too expensive. Most people can't afford PCs and don't know how to use them."[2]

Ellison's idea was viewed as a challenge to Microsoft, a competing software company. Oracle hoped

"THE INTERNET CHANGES EVERYTHING"

Larry Ellison's personal mantra is "The Internet changes everything."

In 1995, when Ellison began championing network computers, only about 9 percent of American households were online. By 1997, that number had more than doubled, to 19 percent.

Computer ownership was even more widespread than Internet access. In 1998, 45 percent of American homes had a personal computer in them. Half of these home PCs were wired to the Internet.

By the end of 1999, there were 259 million Internet users worldwide. By 2002, the number was expected to grow to 490 million.[3] With so many people using this new technology, it was bound to affect their lives in dramatic ways.

that low-cost NCs would catch on with computer users. It offered a machine to consumers at a cost of $199. Full-featured personal computers cost ten times as much.

But NCs did not become popular. "Ellison's view was slow to catch on," the *Industry Standard* wrote in 2001, "largely because the new machines were

A GIANT COMPANY

Oracle Corporation has experienced tremendous growth over the past decade or more. Here's a chart of the company's earnings since 1988:

FISCAL YEAR	EARNINGS
1988	$282 million
1989	$584 million
1990	$971 million
1991	$1.0 billion
1992	$1.2 billion
1993	$1.5 billion
1994	$2.0 billion
1995	$2.9 billion
1996	$4.2 billion
1997	$5.7 billion
1998	$7.1 billion
1999	$8.8 billion
2000	$10.1 billion
2001	$10.9 billion

Source: The Oracle Corporation

slower than regular computers and offered far fewer choices."[4]

Nevertheless, Ellison had the right idea. He was pointing his company in the direction of the Internet. In the mid-1990s, the Internet was becoming a huge part of business and everyday life. Database technology was growing in importance.

"The Internet changes everything" became Ellison's slogan.[5] He transformed Oracle into a true e-business. All of the company's software was redesigned to make use of the Internet. By focusing on the Internet, Ellison was leading Oracle to new heights of success.

This Challenger aerobatic single-engine plane bears the Oracle name and performs at air shows around the country. An active pilot himself, Ellison enjoys flying fighter jets.

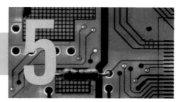

A Global Software Powerhouse

By 2001, Oracle Corporation had become a global software powerhouse, second only to Microsoft. Oracle's annual revenues were $10.9 billion. It employed more than forty-three thousand people.

Oracle's success was based on the basic rule of business: offer a good product at a good price. Oracle's database software handled information at a very high speed. It was reliable, and it was priced affordably. Oracle's success came from two things: its solid database products, and Ellison's focus on the Internet.

"In June of 1999," Ellison said, "we announced that Oracle would become an e-business and, in doing so, would save $1 billion. We would use our own application software—the Oracle E-Business Suite—to put every aspect of our business on the Internet."[1]

Ellison made Oracle an example of how businesses could save money by using the Internet and Oracle software. He hoped that business leaders everywhere would agree with him.

"The Oracle database is already the key software building block of the Internet," Ellison told Oracle shareholders in 2000.

> 65 percent of the Fortune 100 use Oracle for e-business. All ten of the world's largest Web sites, from Amazon.com to Yahoo!, rely on Oracle's ability to handle huge numbers of users and enormous quantities of information—text, images, audio, video—everything.[2]

As amazing as the Oracle story was, the company remained the number two software company in the

UNIMAGINABLE WEALTH

Larry Ellison built an incredible personal fortune by selling his software. When people talk about riches in the computer and Internet field, though, they think of Microsoft's Bill Gates first. Here's a comparison of each man's worth.

YEAR	GATES	ELLISON
1996	$18.5 billion	$6 billion
1997	$39.8 billion	$9.2 billion
1998	$58.4 billion	$4.9 billion
1999	$85 billion	$13 billion
2000	$63 billion	$58 billion
2001	$58 billion	$26 billion
2002	$52.8 billion	$23.5 billion

Source: *Forbes Magazine*

By becoming an e-business itself, Oracle hoped to show other companies how they could save money. By using Internet technology, businesses can increase profits.

world. Microsoft was still in the lead. In 2000, Ellison was the second-richest man in America, behind Microsoft's Bill Gates.

In the world of high-tech business there is no bigger rivalry than the one between Oracle's Larry Ellison and Microsoft's Bill Gates. Ellison has made it no secret that he would like to top Gates's net worth. In 2000, Ellison was the second richest American, trailing Bill Gates by only $5 billion. Ellison was not a man to be content with second place.

"Certainly I want Oracle to be the largest software company in the world," Ellison said. "If I don't, they should get rid of me. That's my job. It's more fun being first than second."[3]

When Larry Ellison co-founded the company that later became Oracle Corporation, he did not know that it would change the way businesses used computers.

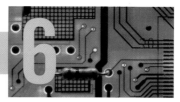

Epilogue

arry Ellison is a self-made man who is larger than life. He is a billionaire businessman who sails yachts, flies fighter jets, and owns a fleet of ultra-expensive cars. His accomplishments in the computing and Internet worlds make him a turn-of-the-century pioneer.

By 2002, Oracle customers included major corporations like the Ford Motor Company, General Electric, Dell, and Hewlett-Packard. Ellison has received many awards for his business leadership, including the Entrepreneur of the Year award from the Harvard School of Business.

Larry Ellison's success has made him very wealthy, and he has used his wealth to help others. In 1997, Oracle founded a program that became known as the Help Us Help Foundation. The Oracle Help Us Help Foundation donates computer equipment and software to schools and youth organizations. Oracle founded Think.com, a Web-based educational

Larry Ellison demonstrates the world's first Internet database software, which allows businesses to store their data on an Internet server. Oracle hoped to show other companies how they could save money by using Internet technology.

experience. Think.com provides teachers and students around the world with free Web pages and learning tools. Oracle also sponsors the Oracle Internet Academy, which teaches high school students computer skills. These efforts are part of Oracle's plan to help make the Internet available to everyone.

One can't help but wonder why Ellison continues to work as hard as he does. Why, when he is one of the richest men in the world, does Ellison continue to run Oracle? Why not let someone else do the job?

"Because," said Ellison, "the more exciting, bigger race is the one that Oracle is in, more exciting than the Sydney-Hobart [yacht race], more exciting than anything I have ever done, is the race toward Internet computing."[1]

Whether Oracle wins the race or gets swamped by the stormy seas of Internet commerce remains to be seen. What's certain, though, is that Larry Ellison has made his mark on the world. His is one of the most remarkable business stories of our time.

CHRONOLOGY

1944 Lawrence Joseph Ellison is born in New York City on August 17.

1962 Ellison graduates from Chicago's South Shore High School and enters the University of Illinois.

1964 Ellison leaves the University of Illinois after completing his sophomore year and enrolls in the University of Chicago.

1967 Ellison marries his first wife, Adda Quinn.

1973 Ellison lands a programming job at Ampex, where he meets his future business partners Bob Miner and Ed Oates.

1974 Ellison and his first wife, Adda Quinn, divorce.

1976 Ellison marries his second wife, Nancy Elizabeth Wheeler.

1977 Ellison, Bob Miner, and Ed Oates create Software Development Laboratories in June.

1978 Ellison and Nancy Elizabeth Wheeler divorce.

1979 The first version of Oracle database software is released in November.

1983 Software Development Laboratories renames itself Oracle Corporation; Ellison marries his third wife, Barbara Boothe.

1986 Oracle becomes a public company on March 12; Ellison and Barbara Boothe divorce.

1995 Ellison champions the idea of network computers.

1998 Ellison competes in the Sydney-Hobart yacht race in December. His yacht *Sayonara* battles extraordinary weather to win, but six men on competing boats die.

1999 In June, Ellison announces that Oracle will become an e-business and save $1 billion in the process.

2000 Oracle launches its E-Business Network.

2001 Oracle sales reach $10.9 billion.

2002 Oracle 9i Database is ranked the number one database server by *PC Magazine*.

CHAPTER NOTES

CHAPTER ONE. High Drama on the High Seas

1. "Larry Ellison's Brush With Death Aboard *Sayonara*," *Business Week.com*, May 8, 2000, <http://www.businessweek.com/2000/00_19/b3680008.htm> (March 20, 2002).

2. "Australian Yacht Race Organizers Announce Inquiry," *CNN.com,* December 29, 1998,<http://www.cnn.com/WORLD/asiapcf/9812/29/aussie.yacht.03> (March 20, 2002).

3. Rob Mundle, "Sydney To Hobart Race: Death and Desperate Moments Subdue Australia's Classic Race," *Sailing World.com,* December 31, 1998, <http://old.cruisingworld.com/gps/1998/gps5398.htm> (March 20, 2002).

4. Rick Aristotle Munarriz, "How Did it Double?" *The Motley Fool,* December 30, 1999. <http://www.fool.com/ddouble/1999/ddouble991230.htm> (March 20, 2002).

5. Andrew E. Serwer, "Larry Ellison Aims For No. 1," *ABCNews.com,* November 1, 2000, http://abcnews.go.com/sections/business/DailyNews/serwer_talk_001101.html> (March 20, 2002).

6. "Larry Ellison's Brush With Death Aboard *Sayonara.*"

CHAPTER TWO. Humble Beginnings

1. Mike Wilson, *The Difference Between God and Larry Ellison (God Doesn't Think He's Larry Ellison)* (New York: William Morrow, 1997), pp. 17-18.

2. Daniel Morrow, interviewer, "Smithsonian Institution Oral and Video Histories: Lawrence Ellison," October 24, 1995, <http://www.americanhistory.si.edu/csr/comphist/le1.html> (March 20, 2002).

3. Ibid.

4. "Q and A: The Oracle Speaks," *Businessweek.com,* February 26, 2001, <http://www.businessweek.com/2001/01_09/b3721108.htm> (March 20, 2002).

5. Wilson, pp. 17-18.

6. "Q and A: The Oracle Speaks."

7. Morrow.

CHAPTER THREE. The Creation of Oracle

1. Mike Wilson, *The Difference Between God and Larry Ellison (God Doesn't Think He's Larry Ellison)* (New York: William Morrow, 1997), p. 42.

2. Daniel Morrow, interviewer, "Smithsonian Institution Oral and Video Histories: Lawrence Ellison," October 24, 1995, <http://www.americanhistory.si.edu/csr/comphist/le1.html> (March 20, 2002).

3. Ibid.

CHAPTER FOUR. "The Internet Changes Everything"

1. Daniel Morrow, interviewer, "Smithsonian Institution Oral and Video Histories: Lawrence Ellison," October 24, 1995, <http://www.americanhistory.si.edu/csr/comphist/le1.html> (March 20, 2002).

2. Juan Carlos Perez, "Ellison Eyes The Future And Sees The NC," *PCWeek Online,* November 5, 1996, <http://www.zdnet.com/eweek/news/1104/05aelli.html> (September 1, 2001).

3. "Worldwide Internet Population," *Commerce.net,* <http://www.commerce.net/research/stats/wwstats.html> (March 20, 2002).

4. Dan Goodin, "Network Computing Lives!" *The Industry Standard,* August 19, 2001, <http://www.thestandard.com/article/display/0,1151,7936,00.html> (March 20, 2002).

5. Bren Schlender, "Oracle at Web Speed: 'The Internet Changes Everything,' and the CEO of Oracle Is Living Proof," *eCompany.com,* May 1999, <http://www.ecompany.com/articles/mag/print/0,1643,4974,00.html> (March 20, 2002).

CHAPTER FIVE. A Global Software Powerhouse

1. Mark J. Barrenechea, foreword by Larry Ellison, *E-Business or Out of Business* (New York: McGraw Hill, 2001), p.V.

2. Larry Ellison, "Letter To Our Shareholders," Oracle Annual Report 1999, <http://www.oracle.com/corporate/annual_report/99/index.html?letter99.html> (March 20, 2002).

3. John Dodge and Wendy Pickering, "Q and A With Oracle's Larry Ellison," *PC Week,* July 24, 1995, <http://www.zdnet.com/eweek/news/0724/ellison.html> (September 1, 2001).

CHAPTER SIX. Epilogue

1. Duncan Martell, "The Silicon Swashbuckler," Reuters, June 29, 2000, <http://www.zdnet.com/filters/printerfriendly/0,6.6061,2596450-2,00.html> (September 1, 2001).

GLOSSARY

browser—The software that enables a computer to retrieve and display documents posted to the World Wide Web.

bug—An error in a computer program.

CEO—Chief Executive Officer; the person in a company who is responsible for the overall activities of that company.

database—Any collection of information organized in a specific, consistent way.

entrepreneur—A risk-taker who starts a new business.

ghetto—A section of a city where members of a minority group live, often because of economic reasons.

hard drive—The "storage area" of a computer; the memory where programs and documents are stored electronically.

initial public offering—The first public sale of stock in a company.

Internet—The worldwide system of connected computer networks. The World Wide Web is part of the Internet.

mainframe—A large, powerful computer, used to handle and store large amounts of information. Much larger than home computers, mainframes are typically used by businesses and governments.

network—A group of computers that are connected so that they can communicate with each other.

operating system—The software that allows a computer to operate and tells the computer how to run other software such as word processing programs and games.

relational database—A database that can store information in multiple tables and create relationships between tables. This allows the user to find and use information in sophisticated ways.

server—A machine that provides services on the Internet.

software—Computer programs that tell the computer how to perform certain tasks.

stock—A share, or portion, of a business that is sold to an investor. When a company sells stock, it gets money to invest in the growth of its business. When it makes profits, it shares these profits with investors.

stockholder—An investor who owns stocks.

stock market—A financial exchange where stocks are bought and sold.

structured query language (SQL)—A special programming language that is used to create relational databases.

FURTHER READING

Berry, Charles W. *Computer and Internet Dictionary for Ages 9 to 99.* Hauppauge, New York: Barrons Educational Series, 2000.

Claybourne, Anna. *Computer Dictionary for Beginners.* London: Usborne, 2001.

Ehrenhaft, Daniel, and Josepha Sherman. *Larry Ellison: Sheer Nerve.* Breckenridge, Colorado: Twenty First Century Books, 2001.

Hjortberg, Charles A. *Kids and Computers.* Edina, Minnesota: Abdo & Daughters, 2000.

Stone, Florence M. *The Oracle of Oracle: The Story of Volatile CEO Larry Ellison and the Strategies Behind His Company's Phenomenal Success,* New York: Amacom, 2002.

INTERNET ADDRESSES

Transcript of a 1995 "Video History Interview" with Larry Ellison, conducted by Daniel Morrow on behalf of the Smithsonian Institution's National Museum of American History.
http://americanhistory.si.edu/csr/comphist/le1.html

Oracle Corporation's official Web site.
http://www.oracle.com

A global learning community connecting students and teachers, sponsored by Oracle.
http://www.think.com

A non-profit organization sponsored by Oracle providing computers and software to schools and youth organizations.
http://www.helpushelp.org

INDEX